MW01295227

Pecan Tree Care

Aguide for growing pecan trees including planting pecan trees, fertilizing and watering pecan trees, small pecan orchard management, and pecan tree care.

By Rodney Strange

About the author

An entrepreneur at heart, Rodney Strange pursued his passion for agriculture with the purchase of a pecan orchard consisting of 120 pecan trees in 1996. With an eye on profitability and business success, Strange began the study of Dendrology, specifically pecan tree management. As his orchard reached peak production age, he then turned to marketing his pecan crop online, shipping Southern Star Pecans worldwide. As the demand exceeded his supply, Strange began purchasing pecans throughout western Texas to meet his customers' demands. With the onset of a devastating three years drought resulting in major setback in his orchard, Rodney Strange made a difficult decision to put his farming interests on a back burner.

Strange would return to his passion of writing, publishing weekly blog posts for several years before leaping into the role of author. Rodney Strange currently has four published novels with a new project underway.

Also by Rodney Strange:

Nineteen Seventy Something

Imperceptible: The Parables of Steele

Available in paperback and Kindle format on Amazon.com

Made in the USA
Columbia, SC
03 July 2025

the type of soil. Your geographic location must be considered. Is your area suitable for pecan production? Once you've settled on location, you need to determine which varieties of pecan trees you want to plant. You will need at least two varieties, compatible with each other in terms of pollination. These varieties must be suitable for your area, and should be able to live up to your expectations. If you wish to produce big pecans, plant a tree that will deliver.

Determine where you will purchase your trees. I encourage you to shop around, not only for the best price, but for the best tree at the best price. Remember a three-year-old tree will produce two years sooner than a one-year old tree. The price difference may be insignificant when you harvest your first crop two years earlier than you would have had you purchased younger trees.

Finally, plan the layout of your orchard. This includes your irrigation system, which in my opinion, should be installed prior to planting your trees, decide as to whether you want to water via drip irrigation or with a sprinkler system. What do I think is best? Actually, probably a little of both is optimal. We use drip irrigation and consistently have bountiful crops of large, well filled nuts. However, I've noticed that our trees seem to put on the most growth during rainy summers, and trees located close enough to our yard to receive the benefit of our sprinkler are noticeably larger than the other trees in the orchard.

Decide how far apart you will plant our trees, keeping in mind that in some far away distant future, they will create a shade canopy of fifty feet or more. The 'nut gurus' have determined that pecan trees must have sufficient sunlight to produce optimally. Thus, while thirty feet was once recommended, we are now told we should plant between fifty and eighty feet apart. I personally would plant forty feet apart which will give you 24 trees per acre

The physical layout begins with yards, if not miles of rope

or twine stretched the complete distance of your intended orchard. With an auger and a measuring tape, begin 'plugging' holes in the earth every forty feet (or whatever you choose.) I suggest you drill all the holes for your trees before you begin planting keeping a distance of at least four feet from any underground irrigation lines. Below are two diagrams for orchard planting. Our orchard is planted using the triangle design, which I personally prefer, and it allows an additional 15% more trees per acre than the square design.

All you have left to do is plant your trees. Sounds simple, huh? The details involved in planting a pecan orchard are too complex to address on this one page. If you are seriously considering such a task, I encourage you to visit with area pecan producers and ask for their advice and input.

I will close with this thought...planting and maintaining a pecan orchard is like investing in the stock market. You must be in it for the long haul. You must be able to invest for years without seeing a return. You must really want to be a pecan farmer, that's it in a nutshell.

I

Growing Pecan Trees - A Homeowners Guide to Pecan Tree Care

When one stumbles across a book such as this, an entire database devoted to the art of growing pecan trees, he/she might draw the conclusion that growing a pecan tree must indeed be one of the most difficult and complicated chores on earth. I assure you it is not true. Pecan trees have

survived and thrived throughout Texas and the southern United States for...well, who knows. Pecans were a mainstay diet for our Native American Indians (I hope I'm politically correct there.)

It is important to note that pecan trees thrived for centuries without special attention only when conditions were right for their survival. The same will hold true with a pecan tree that you plant on your property, or one that you perhaps inherit with the purchase of your property. They aren't the type of tree that you can just ignore like you can that Mulberry tree in your back yard, that, as you are sitting here reading this, is taking matters into its own hands and firmly planting its massive root system into your sewer pipe.

Pecan trees do indeed have a feeder root system that extends underground about as far as its overhead canopy of leaves. While these feeder roots do draw in water and nutrients what will ultimately lead to the success or failure of your pecan tree is how successful its massive tap root is in acquiring a substantial source of water from deep within the ground.

So, rule number one in successfully growing a pecan tree is providing water for it. Raining on your tree, for the most part, doesn't count. A newly planted pecan tree during its first growing season will typically need a gallon of water a day. That means every day, not Monday, Wednesday, Friday, or gee...I forgot. This doesn't mean you have to water every day. It does mean that when you water, be it every seven days, you need to water deeply so the feeder roots can search out and find moisture. And for the most part, the sprinkler watering your lawn will not provide sufficient water for your pecan tree.

If you have a mature tree in your yard, it will need between 100 to 250 gallons of water per day during the hottest part of summer, if it is to provide you with a crop of pecans. When a pecan tree begins to stress, whether it be from

lack of water, an insect infestation, or disease, the first line of defense is to turn loose of its crop of nuts.

So, if you haven't been paying attention so far, thou shalt water thy pecan tree.

With sufficient water and nothing else, a pecan tree will survive. However, if you don't do anything else, such as pruning, your tree will become nothing more than a pecan bush. Pecan trees are lazy trees and prefer to grow their branches close to the ground. It takes less energy to grow branch two feet from the ground than it does way up high. There are no strict rules in pruning and you really can't go wrong unless you just go wild and cut all the branches off your tree. Keep your branches trimmed to the height of you head, or the height of the tallest member in your family. It's that simple. Every spring, your tree will try to be lazy and pop little shoots out all around its trunk. Just pinch them off.

There are some problems you may encounter. Insects can cause considerable damage if not controlled properly. Part of our pecan orchard management program is to NOT just go around haphazardly spraying pesticides 'just because.' There are entire seasons that we do not spray our trees. This should be your policy, also. Spray only when needed, using the least amount necessary to get the job done. If you have a newly planted tree, it is very important to control aphids and other bugs that may 'eat your leaves'...no leaves, no tree.

You can treat most of your insect problems with the usual 'over-the-counter' sprays found at your local home and garden center. The most frequent problem associated with pecan pests is that sticky 'syrup' that just floats through the air and coats your car windshield and everything else. This is caused by aphids, or as the nut gurus have discovered, is a result of Aphids uh...pooping on the leaves of your tree and tiny Micro-organisms feeding on uh...IT, which since IT is on the leaves, result in leaf damage and

the resulting 'floating syrup.' To clear up his problem, simply spray your tree (or your neighbors) with an over-the-counter spray that claims to control Aphids.

Your pecan tree need Zinc and I personally think that it is almost as important as water for your tree. Signs of zinc deficiency are pale green leaves, bare branches with a cluster of small pale leaves at its tip, and dead branches in the tops of your trees. A lack of zinc also prevents nuts from filling out. Zinc is available at most garden centers, either in a liquid or powder form. You should spray the foliage on your trees with a zinc spray three to four times early in the growing season, beginning with leaf bud in spring and regularly every three weeks or so into mid-June. Do not spray zinc during the heat of the day, as it could cause leaf burn.

Fertilizing your pecan tree is necessary to ensure growth and nut production. Ammonium Sulfate is a common nitrogen fertilizer for pecan trees and is readily available at home and garden centers. While the 'nut gurus' have a whole book of formulas and theories concerning pecan tree fertilization, it is usually accepted that for each inch in diameter of tree trunk (a foot above the soil) you should apply one pound of fertilizer. If you don't want to rummage around the sewing box for your wife's measuring tape, you can also apply one pound of fertilizer for each year of your trees age. You should apply fertilizer twice during the growing season, once at mid-March and again in mid-May. So, if you determine you need to apply ten pounds of fertilizer (because your tree is ten inches in diameter or ten years old) you would make two applications of five pounds each. Apply evenly underneath the entire canopy of the tree. I recommend that you water your tree deeply prior to application, then water only lightly to dissolve the fertilizer just beneath the soil. This allows the feeder roots access to the nitrogen over a longer period.

These tips are just a generalization on proper pecan tree

care. For more in-depth and detailed articles on growing pecan trees, be sure to visit our other sections.

Watering Pecan Trees

If you don't do anything else 'by the book' when it comes to caring for your pecan trees, water...water...water.
I will be the first to tell you that it's ok to under-fertilize, to miss a zinc application, to let insects get a little out of hand, but I will not give you my 'thumbs up' when you decide not to water your trees properly. If you water as you should, and do nothing else to your trees the entire growing season, chances are good that you will produce an acceptable pecan crop.
To calculate the amount of water needed, numerous factors need to be considered. Naturally, the size of your tree(s) plays a factor. The time of year, of course must be considered. The type of soil your tree(s) are planted in.
It's a no-brainer that smaller, younger pecan trees will require less water than mature trees, however do not underestimate their water requirements. A mature tree has an extensive root system to harvest moisture from a substantial area while a young tree's roots may only spread two or three feet from the trunk. A safe starting point when determining water needs of a newly planted tree during its first growing season is one gallon of water per day. This is not to say you should pour a milk jug of water on your tree daily, but when you do water (weekly is good for young trees,) water sufficiently to carry your tree through till the next watering. For the first three years of your tree's life, I recommend at least one gallon of water

per day for each year of your tree's age. From age four to age seven, double that requirement, except during the hottest months of the growing season. Then you should double what you just doubled. Lost? At age three, your tree should receive three gallons of water per day. (twenty-one gallons per week or forty-two gallons if you water bi-weekly.) At age four, your tree should receive eight gallons of water per day, except when the temperatures approach ninety-five degrees or higher (or winds deplete the soil moisture.) Once hot weather sets in, your four-year-old tree should be receiving around sixteen gallons of water per day.

By age seven, your pecan tree is beginning to reach 'puberty,' that is, it is in its pre-production stage of growth. Your tree is larger (taller, wider) so more energy is required. Your tree is approaching the nut bearing stage in its life which will require substantial amounts of water. You must now determine how much water it will take to keep the entire area moist beneath the canopy area of your pecan tree...to a depth of four feet. Your initial watering every spring should be a deep watering to saturate the soil beneath your tree. After that, you need to water whenever 60% of the initial water has been depleted. To judge when to water, you must take the soil type into consideration. Sandy soil can only store approximately one inch of moisture per one foot of soil depth whereas clay soils store three times as much. So, if you receive a one-inch rain, and your tree is planted in sandy soil, only the first foot is storing any moisture. It is important to understand that for the most part, rain just doesn't count when you are talking about watering pecan trees.

I think you should get into the mindset that you probably aren't watering your pecan trees enough. A producing pecan tree over the age of ten will need upwards of 150 to 300 gallons of water per day during the hottest part of the growing season. From April thru June, we generally water

our trees ten hours per week. (Our 'drip irrigation' system has been modified to more of a 'water hose running full blast' at the base of our trees.) During July thru September, we water sixteen to eighteen hours per week per tree. When harvest comes, we can still identify trees that didn't receive sufficient water. They may have dropped their nuts early, produced smaller pecans, less pecans, or the pecan hulls failed to open properly (stick tights.)

Whether you are contemplating planting a pecan orchard or purchasing an existing one, water availability should be a major factor in your decision. A pecan orchard must have an unlimited source of water if it is to survive, AND... you must make a commitment to see to it your trees receive the amount of water they will need to produce a sufficient crop of pecans.

Pecan Orchard Irrigation and Alternative Watering Methods

I've been known to say that both drip irrigation and utilizing a sprinkler system are the right way to water your pecan orchard. I'll also tell you they're both the wrong way. Just a year or so after I purchased our orchard, I looked out my front door and say an old man knelt on the ground by one of my trees at the edge of the orchard digging in the dirt. I scurried over toward him and stood over him awaiting some sort of explanation as to what exactly he was doing. Without looking up or even introducing himself, he told me that my neighbor had consulted him about gopher problems and he had decided they were coming from my orchard. As I watched him carefully set a trap, he declared gruffly, "These pecan trees won't never amount to nothin'. You're using drip irrigation...they gotta have a sprinkler system." I coaxed him to divulge his identity and discovered he owned a small five-acre pecan orchard just down the road from me. I had noticed the sprinkler system in his orchard and had caught myself admiring the condition of his trees from time to time as I drove past. The brief conversation left me troubled about my drip irrigation for quite some time. (Somewhere, someday, I'll tell you a funny story about this old man fighting an EMU that wondered up in his orchard.)

I began checking into sprinkler systems and found that they were just too cost prohibitive for our little operation. I also determined that a sprinkler system would be somewhat insufficient and costlier to operate. Between a third to half of the water used is lost to evaporation. At least another third of the water is placed where the trees

cannot utilize it, being in the middle of the tree rows, where tree roots cannot reach it. I also concluded that irrigating the entire orchard would encourage insects to take up residence in the wet soil throughout the orchard and make weed control a huge undertaking. Once I had accepted the fact that my drip system would have to suffice, I began contemplating how I could make it work.

The old man was right, and I knew it. The way our system was set up, water was meant to trickle to all one hundred and something trees simultaneously. It wasn't working. Some trees watered well, while others received no water at all, especially those at the end of the orchard.

I began my modification by removing the emitters from every polyethylene lateral line running to the base of the trees. I then cut the end off the line with a pocket knife. I tested my modification and saw that many of the trees still did not receive water.

The previous owner had come up with an ingenious idea to deliver water to the orchard using the force of gravity. He had constructed a 'water tower' above the well house, a tank holding 2500 gallons of water. A cut-off valve controlled the flow to the orchard through a two-inch PVC pipe which ran two feet below the ground. At each row of trees, a one-inch PVC pipe diverted water down the tree row. The only flaw in the system was insufficient pressure to move the water back up to ground level through the 3/8-inch polyethylene lateral line.

Armed with a plastic bag of PVC elbows, one-inch PVC pipe, ball valves, and a shovel, I set out one spring to overhaul my drip irrigation system. I found the one-inch pipe supplying each tree row and installed a cut-off at ground level. This would enable me to water only one or two rows of trees at a time. After completing my work, I tested the system, and with the new control valves in place and the ends cut off the poly lines, it worked like a charm.

I can't claim to have a drip irrigation system. It's more like

a super-charged flood irrigation system, only we don't flood the entire orchard, just the immediate area around our pecan trees. We have no water runoff, no wasted water, no wasted electricity putting water where it's not needed. Our irrigation system is an energy efficient, natural resource conscious, heck..in my opinion, it's the perfect irrigation system.

So the old man was partly right and partly wrong. A drip irrigation system was obviously not going to do the job, but it didn't take a sprinkler system to make my pecan orchard thrive.

I don't consider myself to be necessarily ecologically minded, but I don't see the need to waste water. At the same time, I fully understand the importance of water to successful pecan production. I also know that out here in west Texas that our trees won't survive if our underground water source is depleted. Matter of fact, West Texas won't survive without water. If you feel you are perhaps pulling more water out of the ground than necessary, if you're watering more dirt than trees, or if you're allowing a substantial amount of water to evaporate before it even hits the dirt...maybe you ought to something about it.

Fertilizing Pecan Trees

I hope you have already read our section on watering pecan trees. Watering and fertilizing pecan trees go hand in hand, and utilizing sufficient quantities of either offsets the need to over-apply the other. This knowledge offers you the opportunity to make some decisions that might make the difference in making a profit or going 'in the hole' from year to year. Before we continue, I insist you read the

section on Zinc application just as soon as you've finished this chapter. Next to watering your pecan trees, there is not a more important chore than applying zinc to your pecan trees...even more important than applying fertilizer! I've not typically been an advocate of over-fertilization throughout the years, basing my beliefs that the world's greenery survived for millions of years prior to the introduction of fertilizers, and did quite well without them. However, fertilizer does have its place in pecan production. I'm going to start by looking at the lawn, yes sir, the front yard. For years and years, I was adamant that my lawn did not need commercial fertilizer, and daily throughout each summer, I would drag a sprinkler around the yard to keep it green. One spring my wife brought home a bag of lawn fertilizer and a spreader and told me to fertilize the grass. (That's how it works, isn't it?) Throughout that summer I found there was little need to water more than once a week, and as a matter of fact, there was little time to water between the bi-weekly mowing chores of our lush green lawn. I now fertilize our lawn yearly.

The same is very true when applying fertilizer to your pecan trees, whether it be a single tree in your back yard, or an entire orchard of pecan trees. Yearly application improves both the number of pecans your tree produces and the size of the nuts. However, if you're a business-minded person, the economics of the process must be considered. The 'experts' (nut gurus) that study the art of pecan tree production recommend we apply un-imaginable amounts of fertilizer to our trees. We must keep in mind that while they are conducting their research, making a profit from their pecan crop is the last thing on their mind. I have read research articles that recommend anywhere between forty and sixty pounds of fertilizer PER TREE. While this may be optimal, it certainly is not in our best financial interest, especially if we have an entire pecan orchard to fertilize. It has been my experience in the past

that supplying ample water to your trees can, to an extent, make up the difference in applying meager amounts of fertilizer. Where we live, the cost of watering is by far less than the cost of fertilizing.

The pecan trees in our orchard are approximately twenty years old, and stand between twenty and thirty feet tall. I plan to apply twenty pounds of fertilizer to each tree this spring, a third of the amount the 'nut gurus' recommend. To compensate for the 'under-fertilization,' I will water, water, water. In the past, this process has resulted in ample crops of pecans, and we have been able to make a profit on our operation each and every year.

What pecan fertilizer to use and how to apply it.

When you research the 'kind of fertilizer' to apply to your trees, you find 10-10-10 or 13-13-13 is the suggested fertilizer. I'm like you, that doesn't help me a bit in knowing what I'm supposed to put under my trees. What you need to know is that pecan trees require NITROGEN to produce their nuts. Finding the right pecan fertilizer is as simple as running down to your local Farmer's Co-op or other fertilizer dealer, and telling them you want AMMONIUM SULFATE, which is typically accepted as a suitable pecan tree fertilizer.   I have purchased bags of Ammonium Sulfate at home and garden centers (Lowes, Home Depot, etc.) but find it to be a lower grade which tends to clump and does not dissolve as it should.) While there are other specially formulated fertilizers available, again, you are looking to make a profit, or at least keep expenses to a minimum. Ammonium Sulfate is available either by the bag or in bulk, which is less expensive. If you decide to purchase your fertilizer in bulk, you need to have a method of transporting it to your trees, as well as a method of applying it to your orchard. Fertilizer facilities typically have commercial spreaders available for lease (or they may let you borrow one if they value your business.) This

solves the transport and application problem. Before you decide on this solution keep in mind that using a commercial broadcast spreader will prevent you from being selective in exactly what you will fertilize. If your orchard consists of young trees, you will fertilize large areas of land between your rows, great for the weeds, not so great for your trees and your pocket book. If you have young trees, you can always dig the lawn spreader out of the shed and simply broadcast fertilizer beneath you tree canopy. This puts the fertilizer exactly where it will benefit the tree. In the early years, when our orchard was young, I applied fertilizer using a coffee can. It works just fine on young trees.

When to fertilize

Again, the 'nut gurus' tell us to make our first application in mid-February. Hummm. Your pecan trees will not burst into spring bloom until... April? Keep in mind that the fertilizer you apply to your topsoil will work its way deep into the soil, beyond the reach of your pecan trees' feeder roots. If you apply fertilizer before the feeder roots have awakened from their winter hibernation, AND then receive a substantial rainfall that leaches your fertilizer deep into the soil, you have wasted your fertilizer and your money. We always plan our first application for somewhere towards the end of March. We purchase our fertilizer, then wait for the weatherman to give us a substantial promise of rain. Our goal is to apply fertilizer just prior to a spring rain (not a promised four-inch downpour, just a nice spring shower.) A second fertilizer application should be planned for mid-May. To be sure we're clear on this, if we decide to apply twenty pounds of fertilizer per tree, we will apply ten pounds at the end of March and another ten pounds at mid-May. I do not recommend fertilizer application past May. The chance of it causing damage at this late date outweighs the benefits of the nutrients it provides. Keep in mind-this is typical for West Texas pecan production.

These timeframes may or may not apply for wherever you are located.

Pre-fertilizing preparations and post-fertilization maintenance

To get the 'most bang for your buck,' we suggest you plan your fertilizer application to maximize effectiveness. Just prior to the application, I recommend you water your trees deeply. The purpose is to provide them an ample supply of water to maintain their needs for a few weeks. Once you apply fertilizer, water only lightly to dissolve the fertilizer into the soil (thus the spring shower we try to plan around.) For the next two to three weeks, maintain a light watering schedule to prevent your fertilizer from leaching beyond the reach of the trees' feeder roots, and to allow the roots to absorb as much of the nitrogen as possible. Beyond the three-week timeframe, it will be necessary to resume a regular watering schedule to supply the needed moisture to your tree. Fertilizer application will not only encourage your pecan trees to grow, but will spur weed growth beneath your trees. This is where orchard floor maintenance becomes an important part of your program. Be sure to visit our section on maintaining your orchard 'floor' for specifics and its importance.

Summary

I firmly believe that pecan tree fertilization is indeed a necessary part of your orchard maintenance. It will result in satisfactory tree growth, a larger crop of pecans, and larger pecans. However, it is possible to 'cut corners' in fertilizer application if the need arises. Decide what your budget will stand and still provide you with an acceptable profit. If you can afford to apply sixty pounds of fertilizer to your mature pecan trees, then do it. However, if you are going to have to skip a mortgage payment to fertilize your

orchard, you may be better off cutting back on your fertilizing procedures. It is my opinion that under-fertilizing is the lesser of the evils when it comes doing whatever it takes to make your pecan orchard profitable.

Applying Zinc to Pecan Trees

If you do nothing else to care for your pecans trees, water them regularly and apply zinc applications throughout the early growing season. It is my firm belief that there is nothing more important if you are to achieve a successful pecan crop year after year.

There are two methods for applying zinc, one is what I believe the correct method, the other I believe is the wrong method. The 'nut gurus' for the most part tell us we can either apply zinc sulfate to the soil beneath the tree or apply it to the leaves in liquid form. I suggest you forget about dumping zinc on the ground, probably a useless and money wasting process, and spray your tree foliage with zinc, what I call 'Zinc-ing the trees.'

To zinc your pecan trees with my preferred method, you will, of course, need a sprayer of some sort. If you have only a few trees, or if you have a whole orchard of young, small trees, you may opt for an inexpensive pump sprayer although sooner or later, you will find it necessary to 'move up' to a more efficient and easier to use mechanical sprayer. I personally attempt to run my pecan operation in 'the black' and therefore, have generally worked my way up to larger equipment only when the profits from my orchard permit me to 'pay cash' for equipment improvements.

Whatever sprayer you choose to spray your zinc with, keep

in mind that you will either need a high volume of pressure to reach to top parts of your pecan trees or will need 'some height' to elevate you and the sprayer to a level of your trees' branches. If you choose a smaller sprayer, you may find that riding in the back of a pickup up and down your orchard rows will work nicely. I rig my sprayer onto our old Farmall 560 and take off down the rows, spraying each tree with a zinc solution.

Ah yes, the zinc solution. Zinc Sulfate can easily be found at most home and garden stores in quantities as small as one pound. It is a powder that dissolves well in water, and a little goes a very long way in terms of applying it to your trees. Liquid Zinc is also available. However, it tends to crystallize over a period of time and I've found myself discarding jugs of zinc. I personally recommend the powdered zinc because of this.

Symptoms of zinc deficiency

To spot zinc deficiencies, look for small leaves which curve or curl, leaf edges that are 'wavy,' discoloring in the 'veins' of the leaves, and most noticeable from a distance, long bare branches with small 'clumps' of leaves at the top, or even dead branches with no leaves. Signs of zinc deficiency in the nut are poorly filled kernels and ' hollow pecans.' However, I assure you if you adopt a pecan orchard management program that includes regular zinc applications, you will not find these symptoms in your orchard.

When to apply zinc

Since we've decided to apply zinc directly to the leaves of your pecan tree, obviously the first application must wait until the spring leaves have appeared. Apply your first application when your trees 'look like' they have leaves on them. Pecan leaves appear first as light yellow-green

foliage. This is the optimal time to make the first application. Avoid spraying your trees in the heat of the day since the zinc tends to 'burn' the leaves. Mix your zinc solution according to directions on the package and spray the entire tree until you see 'it raining' beneath your tree. (Maybe just sprinkling.) In other words, coat the leaves of the tree sufficiently for some of the zinc solution to drip from its leaves.

Additional zinc applications should be made every two to three weeks until the first of June. These early season applications should be sufficient to supply your trees' zinc requirements. If you determine your orchard requires pesticide treatment, most pesticides can be mixed into your zinc solution and applied concurrently.

Summary

Zinc applications must be at the top of your list of priorities when it comes to pecan orchard management. Not near enough attention is given to the importance of zinc in the production of pecans. Zinc is an inexpensive and easy to apply nutrient, and the benefits reaped are more than worth the expense and time it takes to supply your pecan trees with one of the best-kept secrets to pecan production success. Zinc your pecan trees!

Pruning, trimming, and training pecan trees

Pruning your pecan tree(s) is a necessary and on-going chore that begins with the initial planting of your tree. Pecan trees are 'lazy' trees and will grow into gigantic 'pecan bushes' if annual pruning is not performed. The goals you seek to achieve in pruning are to encourage upward growth, lateral growth that will allow your tree full

advantage to sunlight, and improved tree management. You also want your trees to well...look nice?

Suckers (small branches) growing along the trunk) will rapidly grow into unmanageable limbs while growth in the upper areas of the tree will stall. It takes less energy, water, and nutrients to promote growth lower on the trunk, thus if lower branches are allowed to remain, the pecan tree will be content just being an unsightly and unmanageable 'bush.'

You can't hardly 'mess up' when it comes to pecan tree pruning unless you (a) don't prune at all, or (b) you prune too heavily. Since you are reading this page, I assume you intend to prune so we'll move on to (b) pruning too heavily. Unless your tree has reached near death and severe pruning is your only hope to revive it, you should never remove more than one-third of its branches in a season. If you follow a yearly pruning schedule, you should never have to prune even that severely.

We bought our pecan orchard when the trees were five to six feet tall. They had been neglected for several years and had branches growing on the lower trunk. With the hope (and the notion that those lower branches produced pecans, too) that we could turn a profit from our pecan crop, or at least break even, we were cautious with our pruning for the first several years. We 'worked our way up' the tree for the first three years, removing the branches from the ground to a height of three feet the first year and removing another two feet of growth each of the following two years. This prevented throwing the trees into shock and allowed top growth to offset the lower branch removal. We were successful in producing a crop each year by following this method.

Pruning is in fact training your tree to grow the way you want it to grow. Pecan trees must have ample sunlight to produce a crop. With this in mind, you should prune to allow the upper branches to spread and to take in as much

sunlight as possible. Many pecan experts say a single vertical trunk is essential. We pruned our trees to achieve this, for the most part. We pruned one tree close to our house into a 'vase' shape because we designated it the 'climbing tree.' Approximately two feet from the ground, it splits into three 'trunks' forming the vase shape. It is a beautiful and well-proportioned tree, and our kids have always claimed it as their tree. So, when it comes to training a young tree, you can decide whether to prune to make it become 'just a tree' or make it an eye-catching part of your landscape. Just be sure you start out with a plan and carry it out throughout the years.

While mature trees will require annual pruning to an extent, your major pruning comes during the first ten to fifteen years of the pecan trees life. Keep in mind during those years that you need access to the orchard floor beneath your tree. You will spend considerable time underneath your tree, watering, fertilizing, controlling weed growth, and oh yeah...picking up pecans. When you are able to prune your tree's lowest limbs to a height just above your head, your major pruning chores are almost finished. There should be no need to prune the lower branches any higher than your head. You might keep in mind that someday you may be bringing in the heavy equipment (harvesting equipment) and be sure the shape of your trees will accommodate these machines. Other than that, your biggest pruning chores are complete.

Mature pecan trees will inevitably require annual attention. Small branches will grow downward in search of sunlight, and limbs bearing a heavy pecan crop will droop and continue a downward growth. The removal of these branches should be the only pruning you will need to perform on mature trees. Again, your goal is to be able to walk beneath your tree without a branch scraping your face!

Occasionally an upper branch will die and need to be

removed. I suggest you purchase a telescoping tree saw/lopper to handle these problems. The cause of these higher branches dying range from high wind damage, freeze damage, disease, and improper care of your tree. I highly suggest you remove any dead limbs from your pecan tree as soon as possible to avoid the possibility of disease spreading throughout your tree.

When to prune your tree

It seems that there is a misconception that pecan trees should be pruned in the dead middle of winter. I personally think this is one of the biggest mistakes you could make. Pruning during the frigid winter months leaves a wound that is exposed to the harsh winter elements. Those who practice this method say there is less chance for insect damage, however, that gaping wound you inflicted on your tree is still present when the bugs do come out in early spring. I recommend you do not prune until early spring, prior to bud break. We plan our pruning for late April, after the leaves have sprouted. This enables the tree to immediately begin its healing process. Pecan trees can be pruned at any time without major setbacks. I discourage summer pruning unless it consists only of small branch removal.

We try to coincide our pruning with the expected crop-set. Pecan trees tend to produce heavily every other year, followed by an 'off year.' We will do our heaviest pruning on our 'on ' years, and prune lightly on our 'off' years. This aids in balancing out our crops and to an extent prevents the tree from stressing from a heavy crop, which would lead to a light crop the next year.

Pruning Tools

If you practice annual pruning faithfully, a pair of hand-held pruning shears should be all you ever need. They fit in

your back pocket and you can continually lop off those small low hanging branches as you tend to your orchard throughout the spring. You may need a larger 'two-handed' lopper if you allow a branch to grow out of control. If you really neglect to prune regularly, you may find a bow saw handy, however, I warn you, pecan wood is an extremely hard wood and will require some muscle to saw a large limb. Somewhere along the way, you will probably decide you need a chainsaw to handle those large limbs. I do recommend you purchase a telescoping tree saw/lopper to reach the highest branches of your tree.

Pecan Orchard Floor Maintenance and Management

Providing proper care for your pecan trees goes beyond maintaining your trees. The ground beneath your pecan trees also requires constant attention. Managing your orchard floor properly alleviates many problems for your trees.

I'd like to address the 'till or no till' controversy. It is typical orchard practice in this area to 'break the ground,' keep the orchard floor plowed and disked. I hesitate to declare this practice 'totally wrong' but I feel it may be a contributing factor to several problems that must be dealt with in the aftermath. When I purchased our orchard in the mid-nineties, I decided not to till based on one sole factor: the West Texas wind. Our house sits within the pecan orchard, and I could not imagine trying to live in the center of a plowed field with the common thirty to forty mile an hour winds. In the spring there is plenty of dust flying around West Texas without me making a contribution. In the years since, I theorize that there may be several benefits to leaving the orchard untilled.

Of course the obvious in our situation is preventing soil erosion. I see orchards throughout this area that are tilled and the most noticeable difference between those and our orchard is the exposure of tree roots, a sure sign of ongoing soil erosion, or more aptly called in west Texas, 'soil displacement.' Orchard tilling also runs the risk of feeder root damage. A tilled orchard is an open invitation to a host of insects, including the most feared in the pecan industry, the pecan weevil, who resides in the soil during the winter and comes out to spread its damage to your trees just as soon as...you till in the spring? I could ramble

on about the till or no-till controversy, but I think I'll end it with "WHY?" I suspect it is the farmer in them...they just feel the need to 'go plow something.'

If you choose not to till your orchard floor, you will probably find yourself mowing. (And some of you now ask, WHY?) I'll head the debate off with the thought that it probably takes the same amount of fuel whether you're mowing or plowing your orchard. Besides, our orchard looks sharp just after I mow, like a golf course with trees. We'll come back to the mowing, but first discuss weed control.

Orchard Weed Control

Weeds will grow whether your orchard is tilled or not, and they must be controlled. Vegetation beneath your trees rob them of needed moisture and nutrients and provide a hiding place for insects. If left uncontrolled, weeds will take over your orchard. An herbicide will solve weed growth beneath your trees. We've used various 'weed killers' and have found Round-up to work longer for us and be the best value for our money. I suggest if you wish to use this brand, you purchase the strongest mixture available. If you are able to buy the 'industrial strength' from a local chemical dealer, (gotta get a license for it in Texas,) go for it. If you must use the 'over-the-counter' stuff, get the super strength. (I don't have any for reference at the moment...purple label, a thick syrupy liquid.) We purchase it by the gallon at Sam's Club for around a hundred bucks and one gallon will just about get us through an entire season.

You will need a sprayer to apply your herbicide. If you use the same spraying equipment for pesticide and zinc application, you must clean your sprayer after spraying your herbicide. Spraying Roundup on the leaves of your trees would be devastating. Our most valuable piece of equipment in our orchard is our garden tractor. It is small enough to carry us beneath the trees and with a small

trailer, can be a workhorse and a time saver. We rig our 25-gallon sprayer onto the trailer and take off up and down the rows, spraying our weed killer. I suggest you kill all vegetation beneath your tree as far out as your canopy of branches reach. Choose a calm day (a challenge in West Texas), and a time that the weatherman promises to be dry and warm. Use caution when applying herbicide and avoid getting any spray on your trees' leaves. Within seven to ten days, your herbicide should have done its job and you should have a neat weedless circle beneath your trees. Typically, an application tends to last a month to six weeks. Then you will need to repeat the process. For our small 100 tree orchard a twenty-five-gallon mixture will treat the entire orchard, with a little left for the weeds around the barn and well house.

Orchard Floor Management
With the weeds under control beneath the canopy of our trees, we now need to deal with the remaining vegetation. In our operation, this is a two-step process. Using our trusty garden tractor, we mow up and down the tree line as far out as our tree branches extend. You can see the need for a clean, rock free and limb free orchard if you are going to set out into the orchard with the lawn mower. Once we have mowed beneath our trees, we crank up the Farmall 560 and head into the orchard with the shredder. It is very feasible to mow the entire orchard with a garden tractor if you don't have access to larger equipment. Our garden tractor has a mowing deck of 42 inches and our shredder mows a 48-inch strip, so we gain very little time in using the shredder...but using the big tractor is maybe 'just a farmer thing?' The entire process of keeping the vegetation under control in our orchard consists of around four hours, and depending on how often you receive rainfall, may need to be done anywhere from a weekly basis to only a few times during the season. This should

be all the orchard floor maintenance   required during the summer months.

As harvest season approaches, you will need to make plans to accommodate whatever method of harvesting you utilize. If you have utilized the till method for your orchard, you will now find it necessary to level your floor by blading or similar procedures. If you use the no-till approach, preparation is as simple as keeping any broken branches and other debris picked up out of the orchard. You may have some 'early-drop' stick tights fall to the orchard floor beginning in late August through September. These should be removed from the orchard as soon as possible as they provide an excellent refuge for pecan weevils. Some of these stick tights may contain Pecan Case bearers who are eager to work their way out into your orchard and begin infesting your crop of pecans. It is extremely important to get anything that doesn't belong in the orchard out prior to the fall nut drop.

Fall Maintenance

A whole new challenge arises as your pecan crop begins to mature and approaches harvest. The leaves from your pecan trees will inevitably fall either before or during nut drop. A good stiff northerly wind usually takes care of our leaf removal out here in West Texas, however we have found it necessary to handle this problem on our own. A gas-powered leaf blower is an invaluable piece of equipment when preparing for the fall harvest. A blower will move leaves, hulls, small branches, and debris away from the base of your trees, leaving a clear area for your pecans to fall into. I highly recommend you maintain a clean area around your trees as you prepare for the nut harvest. It will speed up your harvest process tremendously when that time arrives.

Some Things To Ponder

I receive this question quite often since we also maintain a small herd of goats. Can goats be used in the pecan orchard? I cautiously answer 'yes' if you maintain control. Goats are an excellent form of weed control, however they prefer to eat the leaves on your tree. Old Billy goat will rub his horns on your tree trunk, and could rub the bark off the tree, which will result in death to your tree. Goats love pecans even more than pecan leaves, so they most certainly need to be removed from the orchard prior to nut drop.

If you have a young orchard with lots of 'wasted space' between rows, it is feasible to plant a ground crop of hay grass or something similar. Some pecan producers plant legumes in their orchard to provide a natural source of nitrogen, but we must keep in mind that other crops will tend to compete for water and will provide a breeding ground for insects.

Summary

In this day and age, agriculture producers often 'take the easy route' by over-reliance on pesticides, herbicides, fungicides, and yes, even fertilizers in maintaining their crops. When it comes to pecan production, use of many of these expensive and often somewhat dangerous chemicals can be minimized or even eliminated by proper, natural, and organic orchard management procedures. By managing your orchard floor, controlling weeds, eliminating hiding places for insects to breed and reproduce, and removing any insect or disease infected debris, you can produce a more profitable pecan crop...more efficiently.

Pecan Insect Pest Control and Prevention

Pest prevention is by far more cost effective than pest control. I questioned my knowledge and expertise in this subject prior to offering my advice because we simply have not had a major insect pest problem to deal with in all our years of orchard management. With that said, let's take a look at insect prevention vs insect control.

With the exception of an occasional outbreak of aphids, we have never had a need to launch an all-out war on bugs. I attribute this to several factors. First, our orchard is located in West Texas, a dry area, to say the least. When Georgia's record pecan crop of 2007 flooded the market, they claimed it was due to extremely dry conditions that kept their insect problems to a minimum and allowed for a more marketable crop of pecans. Even though your pecan trees may be in a dry geographic area, the methods you choose to irrigate could produce favorable conditions for insect breeding. I personally am not a fan of sprinkler irrigation. Besides the fact that this method spreads water to areas of your orchard that simply don't need water, sprinkler irrigation undoubtedly contributes to insect infestation. I also believe that tilling your orchard provides easy access for those insects such as the pecan weevil that reside through the winter months in your soil. Practicing good orchard floor management is a key to insect

prevention. Keeping debris, limbs, leaves, and especially those 'early-drop' stick tights picked up eliminates a breeding ground for next year's crop of insect pests. Removal of dead or broken branches from your trees is just as important. Last, but not least, be cautious with what you allow to come into your orchard. Pecans, pecan equipment, or anything else that may have been exposed to a pest infestation at another orchard could import eggs and larvae into yours. I attribute these practices of pest prevention to our lack of insect pests throughout our orchard.

It's important to note that most insects that prey on pecan crops are probably in your area. When aphids magically appear in your orchard after a mid-summer rain, they didn't fly up from East Texas. They've been over at your neighbor's orchard all summer, you know, the guy that's slinging water all over his ten acres with his sprinkler system. Pecan weevils are supposedly isolated to specific areas of Texas However, I suspect that the only main difference between a pecan weevil and the infamous boll weevil that plagues the cotton farmers is what they're laying their eggs in cotton or pecans. The point is...those pecan pests are out there.

If and/or when insect prevention fails, insect control must be implemented. My philosophy is this...use the weakest insecticide needed to get the job done only when it becomes inevitable that your pecan crop is at risk. We do not just go around spraying insecticide 'just because.' There are entire seasons that we do not spray at all. The 'nut gurus' eagerly provide us with information on what to spray and when, regardless whether any insects are present or not.

Keep in mind that producing a profit is apparently the last thing on their minds. Insecticides are expensive...and somewhat dangerous. I believe a healthy pecan orchard can thrive even with the presence of insect predators. When the need does arrive to utilize an insecticide, choose one that will accomplish your task with the minimal amount of risk and with the least expense. When those aphids show up in August, I run down to Walmart and pick up whatever they have available that claims to control these bugs. Last year I spent a total of eighteen dollars and some change on insecticides for our orchard. I personally never spray any insecticides later than August for safety's sake. After all, someone will be eating your pecans.

Insecticide Application for Backyard Trees and Small Orchards

Choosing an effective insecticide can be a simple procedure, especially since there isn't many over the counter solutions available to choose from these days. The insecticides I have found to be effective have become unavailable for most of us. I found Dursban to be the best all-around insecticide, but 'those who know best' have taken it away from the general public, and have since pulled many other effective insecticides off the shelves. Still there are some pest control products available that will keep insects at bay. Read the label and see if a spray will work on your 'bugs.' Keep in mind sprays such as Malathon and Liquid Sevin must be sprayed 'on the bug' to be effective. When shopping for an insecticide, look for those claiming to be effective for a

longer period of time. If you wish to 'stay organic,' you can spray your pecan trees with a soap solution or a mixture including jalapeno or habanero pepper juice.

You will have to have a sprayer capable of reaching the uppermost parts of your tree. Insecticides can usually be combined with your Zinc applications, cutting down on the time you spend spraying your pecan trees. Of course, you should choose a time when no rain is in the forecast and a calm day to prevent spray from drifting. Again, don't spray until you see a definite need to do so. I can tell when it is time to spray for aphids without ever walking out into the orchard. Those pests attack the grapevine in our backyard long before they pose a threat to our pecan trees, and that 'sticky mess' they create on the windshield of my pickup and patio furniture alert me that it is time to spray. Thus, when we do apply insecticide to control aphids, we spray all the vegetation on our property. Otherwise, that grapevine (and Mama's flowers) will cease to exist.

Insecticide Application for Larger Orchards

If you have a large pecan orchard or even a small orchard of large trees, it will probably be necessary to bring out the 'big guns' to control insect infestations. The same rules regarding insect prevention still apply and will make a noticeable impact on your insect problems and your bottom line profits. However, a backpack sprayer and a bottle of bug spray from Walmart isn't going to get you very far. Commercial spray equipment will be necessary and commercial pesticides will be needed. Both require a substantial

investment. Utilizing commercial agriculture pesticides in Texas will require an Applicator's License and a training course on how to use these chemicals properly and safely. I know there are some of you out there that 'know somebody' who can get you these chemicals. Be very cautious if you choose to take this route. I know cotton farmers who would probably 'fix me up' but I am also aware that cotton is not an edible commodity whereas pecans are. What may be safe for cotton could be deadly for a food crop such as pecans. I see cattle and goat herds throughout our area grazing on cotton burs dumped in the pasture and wonder if these toxic pesticides are making their way into our food supply through the meat we purchase at the local supermarket. I certainly would not want to be responsible for shipping my pecans out across the United States if there was a chance they were toxic. E-coli outbreaks in spinach and other commodities make national news. It's just a matter of time before a pesticide poisoning makes the evening news. Be responsible...and be cautious.

Summary
Unless the survival of your pecan orchard is in jeopardy, application of pesticides should be based solely on economic variables. If you determine that the loss of pecans due to insect damage will be substantial in a financial sense and that the expense of pesticide application is sufficiently justified to offset these losses, then an insect pest control program is a crucial factor to successful pecan production. However, to minimize insect infestation which in turn

minimizes unnecessary operating expenses, proper orchard management including pest prevention must be exercised on a day to day basis.

Pecan Pest Control-Birds, Squirrels, and Other Varmints

I can always tell when the pecans are ready to harvest without ever stepping out into the orchard. Quite simply, the pecans are ready when the crows show up. I'll bet you read our section on insect control before you landed on this page. We as pecan producers tend to be caught up in insect damage control, while losses resulting from birds, squirrels, deer, and other pecan pests can be far more damaging to our bottom line. My advice to control losses from these predators is this...get your pecans harvested and out of their reach as soon as possible...if at all possible.

Crows, Blue jays, and Such
One crow can consume and/or damage fifteen pounds of pecans per month, and these predators tend to show up by the hundreds just as the hulls begin to split and expose your pecans. It is hard to imagine that a minor insect infestation could come close to causing the monetary losses that these birds inflict upon us. Crows are highly intelligent creatures and can be a challenge to control. However, their intelligence can be used to our advantage. Quite often I find myself stepping out onto the front porch and screaming at a hundred or so crows making my pecan crop their morning snack. For the most part, my vocal threats go unheeded. If I step out and cock my shotgun, however, the entire flock takes to the skies. Old timers swear that if you hang a dead crow from a tree limb, the others will take heed and avoid your orchard. I have seen

this to appear to be effective. Bird cannons, propane-propelled devices that are timed to go off periodically are also effective as long as they work. My young daughter and I built a scarecrow several years ago and as long as I moved it around the orchard every few days, seemed to do the trick. There are various devices available that claim to repel bird predators ranging from plastic snakes to motion detector 'owls.' All of these repellants play on the intelligence these birds possess

.

Squirrels

Squirrels consume even more of your crop, although they typically don't arrive in droves like the crows do. One squirrel can consume fourteen pounds of pecans each month, and they don't wait on hull split. They will begin invading our trees just as soon as the nuts begin to form around the first of September. We do not have a squirrel problem in our orchard. I've seen only one squirrel the entire time we've had this orchard and he must have just been passing through. While a handful of squirrels probably won't make or break you as far as profits go, if you see the need to control these critters, many options are effective. Various traps are readily available, and repellants can be used to discourage these pests. And you can always break out your grandpa's trusty old squirrel gun.

Gophers

While you're wasting ammunition taking pot shots at squirrels, those gophers beneath your soil are busy chomping on your pecan trees' feeder roots as well as gnawing holes in your poly irrigation hose. Destroying your tree roots will inevitably set your tree back and could even kill a young pecan tree. Even more devastating to the growth of your trees is the tunnels these rodents burrow

around the trunk, which will divert water intended for your tree to drain wastefully down the hole. While gopher traps and poisons can be found at most garden centers, we discovered that the addition of a couple of farm cats to our crew completely eliminated our gopher problem.

Rats and Field Mice
These rodents not only carry off the pecans laying around your trees, they will cause considerable damage to pecans you have stored after harvest. Glue traps and poisons are effective, but a few good barn cats are a valuable asset in controlling these pests.

Deer, Goats, and Other Large Predators
While we don't have a problem with deer devouring our pecan crop, we can relate to a 'goat attack' on a pecan orchard. Some years back, a neighbor across the road unloaded a hundred or so goats into his pasture. When I got out of bed the following morning and glanced out the front window, I was horrified to see the entire herd of these 'tree eaters' squirming through a hole in a fence, running across the highway and literally begin devouring our young pecan trees. I made quite a spectacle of myself as I ran out into the orchard wearing only shorts and sandals, so much so that several farmers passing by pulled off the road to watch. Thankfully, they assisted me in running the goats out of the orchard. Even though the neighbor never poked his head out his front door, the goats were gone the following day. Today we maintain a small herd of goats in our back pasture and from time to time they manage to find a way into our pecan orchard. We've found that a good fence and/or a good dog will keep larger pecan predators out of your orchard.

Harvesting Pecans

When to harvest pecans

We'll start with the 'when' and get to the 'how' afterwards. Quite simply, pecans are ready for harvest when the hulls (some people call them 'shucks') begin to split and the pecans start falling to the ground. I always know that pecan harvest will soon be underway when the crows show up and begin snatching the nuts from the uppermost limbs of the pecan trees. The exact timeframe depends on the variety of pecan tree and your geographical location. Here in West Texas, the Western Schley pecans can mature as early as the second week in October, but have clung to the trees up until mid-December. If you live in south Texas or have an early maturing variety of pecan such as Pawnee, your crop could be ready to harvest in mid to late September. The pecans are nearing maturity when the hulls, which have been a crisp green color throughout the summer, begin to show brown stripes where the 'seams' of the hull will eventually appear. You can judge your upcoming harvest date by grasping a pecan hull between your index finger and thumb and applying pressure to the tip. (As if you were holding a syringe and giving a goat a shot.) If the hull splits when gentle pressure is applied, your harvest is likely only a week or two away from beginning. This should be your signal to begin making preparations that will make your harvest easier. During this brief period prior to nut drop, you should clean the area beneath your trees, removing any limbs, early-drop stick tights, rocks, and other debris that will hamper your harvest. If the leaves have begun to fall, removing them just prior to harvest will speed things up considerably. A leaf rake or blower will help in removing leaves from the base of your trees. You should also prepare whatever type of container you will use to

hold your harvested pecans. Those large plastic totes with a snap-on lid work very well. Trash cans or other similar containers work well also. Of course, if you haven't devised a method to use to actually get the nuts picked up, now would be the time to make a decision. And once you've decided how, get whatever tools together to get the job done.

Harvesting Pecans-Your backyard pecan tree

Harvesting your pecan crop can be a time consuming and labor-intensive chore. The procedure can be as simple as grabbing a five-gallon bucket and picking those pecans up one at a time. If you have only a few pecans from a young tree, this process works quite well. If, however, you have several trees, or a large crop from a mature tree, I'd suggest you at least grab a lawn rake and rake those pecans into piles before picking them up and filling your bucket. You bucket will certainly fill up faster! I suggest you have a large plastic tote or two available to put your pecans in, and you might run down to the plumbing supply and purchase a long piece of PVC pipe. You might need it to 'whack' your tree limbs and get as many pecans on the ground as possible before you begin picking them up. The pole won't reach your top limbs, you'll probably have to wait for a stiff north wind to dislodge those pecans, and pick them up later. As I mentioned, the actual act of picking the nuts up off the ground can become quite a chore. There are several ingenious tools available that can make this job easier, ranging from a 'slinky on a stick' up to a nifty piece of equipment that you push like a lawn mower called a 'Bag-A-Nut,' it's plastic tines capturing your pecans and placing them in a hopper. If you have a small tree, or a tree with a small crop of pecans, the 'slinky' will be helpful. If you have several mature pecan trees loaded with nuts, I suggest you invest in the equipment that is made for the business of picking up pecans. Once your

crop is harvested, you will need to store your pecans for a week or two before you take on the chore of shelling them. Pecans straight off the tree will be fresh or 'green' and will not shell easily. Whether you intend to tackle the shelling chore with your hand-held nut cracker, or have them processed at a custom shelling facility, they need to sit and 'cure' for a while and allow the moisture content to moderate. While the plastic totes are handy during the actual harvest process, I really suggest you store the pecans in plastic mesh bags to allow sufficient air circulation. Whole pecans will maintain their quality throughout the winter in these mesh bags if stored in a cool location.

Harvesting the pecans in your orchard
I know of a fella who bought a pecan orchard a few miles away from here a few years ago. The orchard consisted of around a hundred mature trees and sold for a hundred and twenty-five thousand dollars. This individual then went out and bought a hundred thousand dollars of pecan equipment. Two years later, the orchard and the equipment were up for sale for a hundred and twenty-five thousand dollars. Now we don't have to be all that good at math to find out what we can and can't afford to do. One mature pecan tree will produce no more than one hundred pounds of pecans on it's very best year. One hundred mature trees will produce ten thousand pounds of nuts on their best year. If the state of Georgia doesn't produce a single pecan, the very best price a Texas pecan grower can expect to receive for his crop is maybe two dollars a pound. All of that adds up to twenty thousand dollars, and a lot of us know we won't make a hundred pounds per tree, nor will we get two dollars a pound. So, let's get back to harvesting pecans.
When it comes to harvesting your pecan crop, you can choose the hard road and the less costly route, or you can

bring in the fancy equipment that will make harvesting a breeze and with one bad year, send you into bankruptcy. First, you guys with the thousand-acre orchards already have the fancy equipment and know all about harvesting pecans, and I don't even know why you're here. The rest of us, the good ol' boys with five or ten-acre pecan orchards, have to pick up nuts off the ground to make an extra buck or two.

I have to throw this in before we move on. Every single time I pause and stoop down to pick up a stray pecan, I remember a statement I made to my first father-in-law way back when I was young and dumb. I was visiting him one fall around Thanksgiving and we wandered over to a large pecan tree in his front yard. The ground was littered with nuts and the old codger suggested I gather up a sack full and take them home. I sneered and remarked, "I wouldn't waste the effort to bend over and pick up a pecan!" I always get this feeling that he and the good Lord snicker as they peek down and watch me picking up nuts off the ground!

I started searching for a 'better way' to harvest my pecans when our trees were young and dropping no more than five or ten pounds a year. I tried the 'slinky-on-a-stick' tool one year (that was the year I discovered I had arthritis in my hands thanks to that little contraption.) The following year, I bought a shop vac and a converter, so I could run it from my pickup. I spent more time unclogging the hose than I did picking up nuts. I got plans to build a 'pecan harvester' from some guy on E-bay, and discovered I'd need an engineering degree to build it. I toyed with the idea to build a harvester out of a swamp cooler...I still think it might work. Finally, after years of tired, aching bones, I ran across an ad from a company in Florida that builds a harvester that works. They call it the Bag-A-Nut and I endorse it wholeheartedly for those of you who work a small orchard. We use a PVC pole to 'whack' the pecans

from the tree and I built a cleaning table out of a bed frame and mesh wire. All total, including a sprayer, the 'Bag-A-Nut harvester, an old Farmall 560 tractor, and my home-made tools, we have around three thousand dollars invested in equipment.

There are other options available. I understand there is a gigantic pecan orchard out in West Texas with thousands of acres of trees. From what I hear, they employ migrant workers and arm them with yard rakes to harvest their crop. I have a fella come by every year wanting to bring his crew in and 'rake up pecans' on the halves. If your orchard is sufficiently large enough to contract a custom harvester, they will bring their heavy equipment and get the job done in a day. And then there's the equipment you can actually own. There will come a time when our orchard will require more than the 'Bag-A-Nut.' I will not make an investment in harvesting equipment until I can do so profitably. If you choose to purchase your own equipment, I encourage you to start slow, with a piece at a time, and shop around. The cheapest pecan equipment is over-priced so be cautious. I would suggest you purchase a pecan cleaner first. This will save you probably half of your time spent harvesting. A tree shaker will be needed eventually as your trees grow beyond the length of your 'whacking pole.'

Summary

Your annual pecan harvest is, of course, the big event you have worked toward all year long. Timing is of the utmost importance since new crop pecans generally bring a much better price prior to and during the Thanksgiving-Christmas seasons. However, if making a profit from your crop is important, then it is important to make wise business decisions. Purchasing commercial pecan harvesting equipment can be a wise decision. Then again, maybe not. If you are new to pecan production, give yourself a

few years to access your unique situation before jumping in over your head, and deep in debt. After all, a five-gallon bucket makes a great tool in the pecan orchard.

Marketing Pecans

Selling your pecan crop

It's the moment you have waited for all year long, turning your pecan crop into cash. Unfortunately, there are 'forces' out there that are working against you and there are unscrupulous individuals and companies that will take all your pecans and give you very little in return. Let's see what we can do to get more cash for your pecan crop. Receiving a fair price for your pecans starts before the leaves appear on your trees in spring. You can't expect top dollar for your crop if you don't produce top quality pecans. I hear stories from pecan buyers and shellers who pay a fair price for a load of pecans, then discover the shell-out rate is only thirty percent. So, if these buyers gave a grower $1.50 a pound for in-shell pecans and only thirty percent was usable product, they have $4.50 invested in their pecans. That isn't including their cost for storage and shelling, which will more than likely escalate their investment to around $6.00 a pound. They made no money, and that's why you hear stories of pecan growers receiving .40 to .80 per pound. These buyers have been burned time and time again. Therefore, YOU make up your mind that you are going to do everything possible to produce a crop with a shell-out rate of fifty percent or better. That means you have to water, fertilize, apply zinc...the whole nine yards. Fact is, you cannot make a profit selling pecans for less than a dollar a pound.

Commercial Pecan Buyers

These folks have their rules, and if you are going to sell your crop to them, you must follow their rules. Many commercial buyers will not buy less than two thousand

pounds of pecans at a time. They want them clean, free of debris, and bagged. Query area pecan shelling facilities as to whether they buy pecans or know someone who does. If you have a substantial quantity of pecans, they will usually come out and pick them up. They probably will not just drive up to your farm, glance at your pecans, and 'shoot you a price.; Pecan prices are generally derived by a formula called a 'price per point' which is based on your shell-out rate, the pounds of edible nut meat. Other factors influencing this price structure are the color of your nutmeats and the size of the nut. Even though we sell our crop retail straight to the consumer, I have always kept a watchful eye on the wholesale market. It's been my observation that if the market price per point average is $1.50, most growers are receiving between a dollar and a buck thirty-five per pound of in-shell pecans. I personally suggest you know what your shell-out rate is PRIOR to selling your entire crop to a pecan buyer. This puts you in a position to haggle with them when they quote you a lesser price than what the market rate is. Don't lose sight of the fact that these are YOUR pecans. You don't have to sell to the first horse trader...er ah, I meant commercial buyer that comes along.

Forward Contracting

If you decide to get into a 'forward contract' agreement with a commercial buyer, you will have to sell your crop to him. However, when entering into such a contract, you will know how much you will receive for your crop. Producers of large volumes of pecans tend to use forward contracting more than do producers with smaller production. A forward contract is a written agreement between a producer and a pecan sheller relating to the delivery and acceptance of pecans at some future date. Forward contracts specify what the producer will deliver. The shellers promise payment for the pecans, either by specifying the price or how the price will be determined. Shellers usually initiate

forward contracts to assure themselves of enough pecans to supply their customers. Producers benefit from forward contracts by having an assured access to a market, the potential for increased operational efficiency, and reduced-price risk.

Direct Marketing

We chose to sell our pecans directly to the consumer early on in our pecan adventure. We discovered that commercial buyers simply weren't interested in purchasing small quantities of pecans. The first year that we produced a respectable crop, I put a sign down by the road and ran a newspaper ad in the local paper. We had one customer that year. I then realized I was trying to sell pecans to folks that already had a pecan tree in their back yard or lived next to someone who did. Selling pecans in pecan country is like a West Texas farmer trying to sell cotton to his neighbor. "Nope, got cotton over at my place, too." We turned to eBay and found instant success, followed by the realization that the E-bay and PayPal fees were more than the fertilizer and water costs to produce our crop. So, I built a website, then another, and another Back to selling your pecans. If you choose to market them straight to the consumer or even a retail outlet, you will have to work hard to establish your customer base. Check with area bakeries and candy shops, your local grocery store, and anywhere else that may be interested in buying pecans. If you have a brother-in-law that lives 'up north' where pecans aren't available, plan a visit and spend some time trying to establish some connections with retailers in his area that might need your product. You will have to hustle to make this direct marketing idea work. The internet is a great place to market your product and you can do so with or without your own pecan website. There are numerous classifieds sites such as Craig's List and even Facebook, and if you search long enough, there are even 'virtual farmers' markets and such. It's not for everyone, and if

you're producing thirty or forty thousand pounds of pecans every year, quite frankly, it's not the avenue you want to take. This method of marketing your pecans will become a whole different business that will require much of your time to be successful.

Become the Middle Man

If you are producing a sizable pecan crop and you wish to eliminate the middle man, you might consider becoming the middle man. Most commercial pecan buyers are also pecan shellers who have created a wholesale market for their pecans. They can move tons of shelled pecans through their facilities by selling to large food service companies, wholesale and retail outlets, and even exporting pecans to foreign countries. You must take into consideration the expense of purchasing pecan shelling equipment, operating a shelling plant, and the time involved. This marketing channel, called vertical integration, presents an opportunity to enhance your profits as a grower as well as additional income from shelling.

Choosing a Pecan Shelling Facility

It seems that I always have a bitter-sweet relationship with my pecan shellers. Whether you market your entire crop directly to the consumer as we do, or just want to have a few of your pecans shelled for your personal use, the pecan sheller is an important part of your operation...and your success. While I've toned down on my generally negative opinion towards custom shellers, I still have issues with doing business with them.

It must be written in the imaginary 'Pecan Sheller's Handbook' that when you bring your pecans in for processing, they must sit in a dark corner for two, three, or four weeks before being processed. I've taken a load into the sheller and there not be one single pecan in the whole place...and it's still two weeks before I get my shelled pecans back. The fact that it may be two weeks before Thanksgiving and I have a hundred or so eager customers ready to pounce on my new crop of pecans simply does not matter to them. They're not shelling my pecans until they get good and ready. The folks at the shelling facility would tell you that new crop pecans are harder to shell, and if they sit for a while they shell better. They might tell you the new crop of pecans you bring in are green...which means they're FRESH. What they are really saying is that their sixty thousand dollars' worth of pecan equipment can't shell a fresh pecan. I can't make those customers up in Oregon understand that they will have to have their Thanksgiving pecan pie for New Years.

Another issue I have with pecan shellers is the quality of their work. I visited a pecan sheller around the first of October one year, about a month before my crop was due to come off. I walked into his plant and saw at least two dozen or so metal garbage cans with plastic bag liners, all filled to the brim with the prettiest pecan halves I have ever

seen. I asked him about his shell-out ratio and what percentage would be halves compared to pieces. He told me he had brand new equipment and was sure he could turn out 80% halves. The man must have been dyslexic, because when I got my first (and last) batch back from him six weeks later, about 80% were pecan 'crumbs' and the other 20% were pecan halves, and they looked like they had been in a train wreck. Worse than that, the shell-out ratio was only 48%. I know my pecans, I know how to grow them, and I know they will shell out at 55-58% nutmeat.

Which brings me to another issue I feel strongly about. It seems that pecan shellers are obsessed with being **pecan sellers**. That throws up a big red flag for me. That same sheller that botched up my pecans told me that at the beginning of harvest season he was taking in three thousand pounds of pecans per day. I recently read about a custom pecan shelling facility in Oklahoma that took in a quarter million pounds of pecans their first season. Now these folks are charging us between sixty cents to a dollar a pound to shell our pecans. Do the math...that's some big money. Why in blazes do they feel the need to sell pecans...and when do they find the time? Look back up there where I said my shell-out ratio should have been 58% but was only 48%...and I got very few halves back. Now folks, I have had to buy pecans from individuals from time to time to fulfill my customers' requests, and I know first-hand there is not enough profit in it to even mess with it, I only do it to keep my customers happy. So... you read between the lines.

You can pick and choose

I had a business that wanted to purchase one hundred pounds of shelled pecans and give them to their customers for Christmas. I didn't have a sufficient supply on hand, so I ran down to the local sheller with a load. It was early in the season and I know for a fact that he had NO pecans

waiting. I went back a few days later and asked about my pecans and he looked at me smugly and said, 'They're green...I don't want to mess with them.' I went straight back to the orchard, loaded up five hundred pounds and drove forty miles to the next sheller. He did want to mess with them.

You do have a choice. Yes, you might have to drive a way to find a sheller who really wants to do business with you. And you can always use this threat with your local sheller. Pay them a visit prior to harvest and ask questions. What is your typical shell-out ratio? What percentage is halves? How long will I have to wait? Do you re-run the pecans through an Aspirator? What type of equipment do you have? Do you separate the halves and pieces? Will there be any shell left in the finished product? 'I see that you also sell pecans. Where do you get your pecans to sell?' Will I get ALL my pecans back? Will I even get MY pecans back, or some tiny hard-shell natives that you skimmed from someone? Let them know you know what your pecans' shell out ratio is. If you sell directly to consumers, let them know. By all means, let them know that you 'ain't no dummy' and you don't HAVE to give them your business.

The Flip Side

I've been harsh with my above comments concerning custom pecan shellers, though I don't think completely without merit. Not all shellers operate this way. There are some hardworking, honest, folks out there trying to make a living shelling nuts. There are some pet peeves that they have about us also. Let's face it, when you bring in ten or twenty pounds of pecans to shell, it's not worth their time and trouble. They must re-adjust their shelling equipment for the size and thickness of your pecan, and do whatever they must to get a decent shell-out for you. Take fifty pounds in. and make it worth their effort. Remember, I'm the guy who carried five hundred pounds up to the sheller

and is waiting in line while they tinker with the equipment to shell your ten pounds...and I'm the guy who comes nearer paying the bills at the shelling facility. If you have two or three pecan trees 'out back' that you didn't water, fertilize, and zinc all summer...don't expect your shell-out ratio to be more than 30% or so. If that's the best you can do, it's really not worth your money to have them shelled. Take care of your trees! And folks, some of the smallest pecans I've ever seen were at the shelling facility...so small that I wasn't even sure they were
pecans. Can you imagine how difficult it is trying to get nutmeat out of those tiny nuts?

Dear Mr. Custom Sheller

Inevitably there will be some of you stumble across this page. I'm sure all those tacky things I said above are about your competitor, at least I hope so. Mr. Sheller, I want you to know that I need you, that thousands of pecan growers need you...and we do appreciate your being there for us.

More Pecan Information

PECAN VARIETIES SELECTION

There are more than 500 varieties of pecans that have been tried in various parts of the world. Therefore, variety selection is one of the most important decisions a pecan grower can make. Long range performance of an orchard, and the type of management required, is very dependent upon the varieties planted in the beginning. Regular production, disease resistance, tree strength, and nut quality are extremely important in selection of a variety for a specific area. When selecting a variety, the following factors should be considered: Regular production capacity Disease and insect resistance Age tree produces Tree strength and branching characteristics Nut Size Kernel Quality Kernel Percentage Date of ripening Pollination Type Chilling Requirements Most trees which bear early and heavy are slow growing. Because of this, these trees can be planted closer together. Dominant growing varieties grow more rapidly, become crowded sooner, and require thinning at an early age. They begin bearing later in life, make vigorous growth and obtain larger sizes.

POLLINATION

Pecan trees have dichogamous flowering since male and female flowers on a tree mature at different times. If male flowers give off pollen before female flowers are receptive, the tree is protandrous (male first) and is classified as Type I. If female flowers are receptive before male pollen is shed from catkins, the tree is protogynous (female first) and is classified as Type II. When a tree has complete separation of male and female blooms, it must be cross pollinated by another tree. Some pecan varieties have incomplete dichogamy and pollen is given off a brief time during stigma receptive period. In this case, the

tree may be self-pollinated. Self-pollination is undesirable and will reduce nut quality. To insure quality pollination, every orchard should consist of at least 20% of one type of varieties for adequate nut production, except for natives. They are 50% protandrous (Type I) and 50% protogynous (Type II)

PECAN VARIETIES POLLINATION TYPES

Type I Protandrous Pollen first Nutlets last

Varieties Western Desirable Cheyenne - Scab Caddo Pawnee Cape Fear Cherokee - (not recommended) Barton GraCross Brake Clark Moore No. 60 Onliwon Peruque Riverside San Saba Improved Starking Success Oconee Houma - (Looks good - not sure) Creek (15-17 years)

Type II Protogynous Nutlets first Pollen late

Varieties Wichita Choctaw Shawnee Tejas Kiowa Apache - (not recommended) Brooks Burkett Candy Chickasaw - (not recommended) Comanche - (not recommended) Curtis Elliot Evers GraBohls GraKing GraPark GraTex Grazona Hays Ideal Mahan Mohawk Odom Schley Shoshoni - (losing popularity) Stuart Texhan Willmann Sumner Melrose - Bitter taste Moreland

PECAN SOILS

There are two types of soil that are good for pecan production. Alluvial and Upland. Alluvial soil is commonly found in river or stream basins and beds deposited by centuries of overflows over the flood plains of these waters. It is deep, fertile, well-drained and has a good water storing capacity. It also has permanent static water table four feet or more below the surface. Upland soil does not have all the characteristics alluvial soil has for maximum pecan production. Instead, it should have a topsoil that is sandy loam with a depth of 4-7 feet or more. This topsoil should allow fast and easy movement of water.

Another key to good upland soil is the proper makeup of the subsoil. It is necessary to have a permeable, sandy clay subsoil that will allow both water and air penetration. This desired subsoil will be reddish in color, indicating oxidation, blue, slate, and yellow clay subsoils are usually impervious to water and air and, therefore, will not allow root penetration. Pecan Soil Drainage Test Dig a hole 32 inches deep and 8 inches wide. Fill the hole with water (about 7 gallons). Wait 24 hours and check to see if water is drained from the hole. If all is drained, fill again and check in one hour. If all 32 inches are drained in one hour, this means there is more than 32 inches of soil available for pecan production, and the permanent static water table is below 32 inches.

TEMPERATURE

Pecan trees require a mean temperature of 80 degrees F for the three hottest months (June to August) and 45 to 55 degrees for the three coldest months (December to February).

FERTILIZATION RECOMMENDATIONS FOR PECAN TREES

Young non-bearing trees - first year - no fertilizer (2 pound in June if rapid occurs) - Second year - apply 2 pound of Ammonium Nitrate or Ammonium Sulfate in April - 2 pound in May and 2 pound in June S third and 4th year - one pound first of April, May and June S fifth year - two pounds first of April, May and June Bearing Named Varieties and Natives - always follow leaf analysis recommendations Apply one pound of Ammonium Nitrate per inch of tree trunk diameter or 1 2 pound of Ammonium Sulfate per inch of tree trunk diameter Split application: 50% mid-March, 50 % before June Two applications are better than one, three applications are better than two Broadcast around trees canopy to dripline and 10 % more. Available carriers of nitrogen Ammonium Nitrate 33.5 % Ammonium Sulfate 20.5 %

ZINC RECOMMENDATIONS

Young non-bearing trees - apply foliage application every two weeks from April to mid-August Named varieties first spray green tip second spray one week after green tip third spray three weeks after green tip fourth spray Case bearer fifth spray eight weeks after green tip Natives two sprays - first spray - one week after green tip second spray - Case bearer (usually in May) Mix 2 ounce of Zinc Nitrate or Sulfate per gallon of water

MOST HARMFUL INSECTS OF PECANS

Pecan Nut Case bearer - This gray moth is active at night time only and is the most damaging pecan insect pest in Arkansas. Eggs are laid on the tip end of the nutlets. Females lay 50-150 eggs during their five to eight-day life span. Eggs are white when laid, but will turn pink or red prior to hatching. Eggs hatch in four to five days. Insecticides should be applied two to three days after the first eggs hatch. The Case bearer may have one to four generations. By carefully monitoring egg hatch and control of the first generation; the second, third or fourth generation will be controlled. Warm spring temperatures influence Case bearer development. Cool, rainy weather can delay moth activity and egg laying. Thus, the period of egg laying can vary as much as two weeks from year to year. Control – Mother's Day is usually a designated time to start scouting for Case bearer eggs. Insecticides - Check with County Extension Office and refer to MP-144. Hickory Shuck worm - Active mostly at night, over winters as a larva in the shucks of nuts. It begins attacking nuts in early June and continues until harvest. Shuck worms produce three to four generations per year. Control- Emergence of the Shuck worm varies from year to year and orchard to orchard. Spraying should be timed to Shuck worm activity. Activity should be monitored with black light traps. In the absence of a light trap, start scouting for activity in July. Insecticides - Check with County Extension Office and refer to MP-144. Phylloxera -

Leaf phylloxera forms galls on leaves. Nut Phylloxera forms galls on shoots and nuts. Control - Survey trees in May. Mark the trees that have galls on them for treatment the following year. Dormant oil may be applied to trees before bud break in late February and early March. Insecticides must be applied after eggs hatch in spring but before nymphs are protected inside galls. Treat after bud break when leaves are one to two inches long. Insecticides - Check with County Extension Office and refer to Mp-144. -14- Pecan Leaf Scorch Mite - This mite causes >scorch= appearances on foliage. Damage occurs in June, July, August and September, appearing as dark brown blotches on leaflets. Mites usually feed on the underside of leaves, but will feed on the upper leaf surface. In some instances, almost complete defoliation will occur. They over-winter in bark crevices on tree limbs. Life cycle usually is 11-15 days. Control - Thresholds levels not known. Insecticides - Check with County Extension Office and refer to MP-144. Pecan Weevils The Pecan Weevil attacks pecans and hickory prior to shell hardening. Adults will feed on pecans usually causing immature pecan to fall from the tree. Nuts in water stage, if fed on by weevil, will drop prematurely. After water stage during jel stage, female chews a hole through the shell and deposits her eggs inside the nut. After eggs hatch and grub matures, it will chew a hole about 1/8-inch in diameter in the shell and emerge in late September until late December. Control - Control should be aimed at the adult in August. Usually after the first rain occurs, adults will emerge from the soil. Emergence can be determined by shaking lower limbs of tree or setting weevil traps in orchard. Insecticides - Check with County Extension Office and refer to MP-144. Hickory Nut Curculio - This insect causes nuts to abort from the trees. Aborted nuts usually will have a circular puncture in the middle. A brownish liquid seep through the puncture, leaving a syrup-like deposit on the side of the nut. Heavy activity occurs about June 15, and two spray applications

are necessary for control. Control -First spray June 20. -Second spray two weeks later. Insecticides - Check with County Extension Office and refer to MP-144. -15- Yellow Aphids - There are two species of yellow aphids - Black Margined and Yellow Pecan Aphids. They feed on the underside of leaves and generate honeydew while feeding. Aphids can be seen on pecan foliage from bud break to the first freeze, but are usually most abundant and most destructive during August and September. Yellow aphids secrete honeydew, which in turn promotes the growth of sooty mold. The sooty mold (black substance) inhibits photosynthesis. Control - If aphids' population gets to twenty-five or more per compound leaf, a chemical control may be needed. Insecticide - Check with your County Extension Office and refer to MP-144. Black Pecan Aphids - This aphid is more destructive than the yellow aphids. It feeds on the underside of leaves and injects a toxin that causes the leaf tissue between major veins to turn bright yellow. The black pecan aphid also reduces nut fill and lowers production the following year. Control - It is very active in August and September. Treat when aphids average three or more per compound leaf. Insecticide - Check with your County Extension Office and refer to MP-144. Stink-Bugs/Leaf-Footed Bugs - There are three primary types of these bugs - Leaf-Footed bugs, Brown Stink-bugs, and Green Stink-bugs. Adult stink bugs and leaf footed bugs prey on pecans both before and after shell hardening. They are seen on pecan trees late in August and September. Adults over winter in bark crevices, fence rows, and debris. They puncture the shuck and nut shell, and feed on the inner material. Before shell hardening the nuts bleed and abort. After shell hardening, the nuts stay on the tree but there will be small dark spots on kernel. Control-Stink-bugs and Leaf-Footed bugs like legumes (beans and peas, etc.) better than pecans. Plant legumes as a trap crop close to pecan trees and when the bugs invade, control them with a labeled insecticide after the shell hardening stage in September.

Insecticides - Check with your County Extension Office and refer to MP-144.

MOST HARMFUL DISEASES OF PECANS

Pecan Scab - Leaves can be infected from two weeks after bud break until June. Nuts can be infected from May to late September. Lesions are brown and later become black. Lesions reduce photosynthetic activity and cause early leaf loss. Shucks stick to nuts and nuts can become undersized. Nuts may stick to the tree or drop prematurely. Environmental Influences - Frequent rains, high humidity, heavy dew, and cloudy days. Control - Fungicide spray should begin two weeks after bud break. Fungicide - Check with your County Extension Office and refer to MP-154. Shuck Decline - (Shuck Dieback, Shuck Disease, Tulip Disease, etc.) Pecan shuck decline is the collective name for a rash of problems involving the thick outer husk that surrounds a pecan shell. The condition causes the shucks to shrink, blacken and fall before the nuts can fully form. It can cause no kernel, small kernel, blacken kernel, small nuts, stick-tight (shucks stick to shell, etc.). The cause has long been attributed to a fungus, but production stress is responsible. The pecan tree under great production pressure responds by opening its shucks, the tree realizes it=s in trouble and tries to drop its seed to ensure its survival. The condition is worse in prolific varieties, such as Success, Cherokee, Cape Fear and Choctaw. Control - Provide tree with plenty of water in late August to September during kernel filling stage. Stem End Blight The cause of this disease is not known, but it will kill shuck tissue and reduce nut quality. It sometimes appears in August, but more often in September and October. Some nuts on a cluster can be affected while others remain healthy. Stem End Blight begins as a brown or black spot on the shuck near the base of the nut. This black area usually enlarges to cover the entire nut or a least a portion of it. Shortly after black area appears, the nut becomes easily dislodged from its stem. The

earlier the symptoms appear in the season, the poorer the kernel will be. Fungicides - Check with your County Extension Office and refer to MP-154. -17- Vein Spot Vein spot, a foliar disease, is caused by the fungus Oniomania Nerviseda Cole. The fungus over winters in infected leaf debris on the ground. From spring through August, spores are released immediately after rain showers. The greatest spore release usually occurs from late April into early June. Symptoms - Vein spot lesions on pecan foliage closely resemble scab and must be examined very closely in direct sunlight. Vein spot usually looks shiny or greasy while scab appears dull. On the leaflets, the lesions are always centered on midrib veins. Control - Start fungicide applications in late April to protect the foliage throughout May. Fungicides - Check with your County Extension Office and refer to MP-154. Fungal Leaf Scorch Fungal leaf scorch is one of the major causes of premature defoliation of pecans. It can be mistaken for scorch caused by excessive amounts of Nitrogen and Potassium. Symptoms - Like most fungal diseases, fungal leaf scorch develops most rapidly in wet conditions. It usually appears in July and August and becomes severe by September. The characteristic symptom of fungal leaf scorch is a blackened area on the leaf between healthy and dead tissue. The disease usually begins at the base of the leaflets and advances toward the midvein. The dead areas are deep brown or ash, and there are usually distinctive black zones between the green and dead portions of the leaflet. The disease gradually affects more and more healthy tissue, and the leaflets soon drop from the leaf. As more leaflets drop, eventually the entire leaf will be lost. Control - Fungicides used to treat pecan scab also reduce the amount of fungal leaf scorch, but don=t prevent it. Fungicides - Check with your County Extension Office and refer to MP-154.

Storing Pecans

Pecan nuts harvested in the fall can retain their fresh condition during the next year or until consumed, if handled and stored

properly. Good storage helps keep the pecan's quality. The analysis of a superior quality kernel will give a composition of 73–75% oil, 12–15% carbohydrates, 9–10% proteins, 3 to 4% water, and about 1.5% minerals. A high percentage of oil is indicated by plumpness, crispness, and solidity of kernels, compared with shriveling, sponginess, and hollowness. High oil content, and the fact that it is highly unsaturated (93%), or cholesterol free, is one of the most key factors, along with water and temperature, impacting the storability of pecans. Oil. Because oil content in pecans is high, rancidity can develop at warm temperatures and is more noticeable than in most other nuts. Pecan oil is a mixture of several oils, although oleic and linoleic oils are the two principal ones, usually comprising about 95% or more of total oil. Both the amount of oil and degree of saturation vary with geographical locations. Linoleic acid is the primary chemical component responsible for oxidation and rancidity in pecan kernels. Linoleic acid varies widely in different varieties of well matured and plump kernels, and it also varies from year to year in the same variety. Water. Lowering the moisture content of pecan kernels is a key step for maximum storage life of pecans. Pecans, like many other agricultural products, are harvested at moisture contents higher than those required for storage. Pecans harvested early can contain 25–30% moisture. Water content decreases in pecans harvested later in the season. Pecans should be stored at a moisture content of about 4%. Pecan moisture needs to be decreased as soon as practical after harvesting. This prevents molding, discoloration, and breakdown of the oil. Drying pecan nuts was originally done outdoors, by air and sun drying. This process took three to four weeks and molding often took place in the pecans. Artificial drying or drying with forced air is now used for pecans, speeding up the process considerably and eliminating molding problems. Shelled pecans stored at non-freezing temperatures should be maintained in an atmosphere of about

65–70% relative humidity to hold the 3–4% moisture content. Humidity above these values can cause kernel molding and pecan texture deterioration (pecans become soft and rubber-like), whereas lower humidities will cause excessive drying. In-shell pecan kernels will darken under high humidity as a result of the tannic acid being dissolved from the shell lining. For vacuum or gas packed pecans, or those stored under freezing conditions, relative humidity control is not necessary. Temperature. Lower temperatures usually result in longer storage life of nuts. Storage temperatures and predicted storage times of shelled and unshelled pecans are listed in table 1. Pecan pieces have a shorter shelf-life than pecan halves. This time reduction is in proportion to the surface exposure of the pieces. Storage of nutmeat pieces should be limited to 1 or 2 months at temperatures about 32°F. The greatest benefit of storing at low temperature is retention of fresh flavor, followed by color, aroma and texture. Because pecan meats absorb odors and flavors readily from the surroundings, a storage area free of odoriferous materials and commodities is necessary. Even faint odors of paint, wood, asphalt, vegetables, and other fruits can accumulate and appear stronger in the nuts than in the surrounding environment. In-shell pecans can remain good for 4 months at 70°F, but can be stored successfully for 18 months at 32°F to 36°F. Storage life of in-shell nuts may extend to 5 years or more when stored at 0°F

Pruning and Thinning Pecan Trees

There are currently two or three main schools of thought concerning opening up more sunlight to trees in the orchard. All agree that there comes a time when it is necessary to take steps in this direction in order to improve pecan production in almost every orchard. It is commonly accepted that 50% of the orchard

should be covered with tree canopy and 50% should have sunlight reaching the orchard floor. This goal can be reached through selective limb pruning, alternate row thinning, or selective thinning. Selective limb pruning involves creating an imaginary box around the pecan tree with the bottom of the box at a level high enough for sprayers and equipment to pass below. The top of the box will reach 30 ft. above the bottom of the box and the sides of the box will extend ½ way to the trees on all sides of the one being pruned. Any limb extending outside the box should be pruned back to an intersection with another limb within the box and removed without leaving a stub. Only one to three limbs are removed from a given tree at a time. This will help distribute energy into the remaining limbs and will mold and hold the tree within manageable dimensions for spray coverage. This is probably the most conservative method of opening up the orchard to light for those who are hesitant to remove entire trees. However, bear in mind that it is very labor intensive and may be costly. Alternate-row thinning is a common method of getting light to the orchard. This involves removing every or every other tree (depending on age of the orchard) on alternating rows, usually on the diagonal. Removing every tree in alternating rows takes out ½ the trees, while leaving them in a square, although the orientation is rotated 45°. This type of thinning normally results in a loss of yield per acre for the first few years after thinning, but the loss will normally be made up in succeeding years. Alternate-row thinning is the most aggressive manner of opening up light to the orchard and does not take into account the yield potential of each tree and will undoubtedly remove some high yielding trees. Selective thinning is probably the most efficient method of bringing light into the orchard but can be complicated, labor intensive, and requires knowledge of the orchard and individual trees. This method was developed by Dr. Bill Goff at Auburn University and has been used with success in many orchards.

Trees are individually rated by making a visual assessment of a tree's profit potential. This is determined by yield, pest pressure, nut quality, and value. Variety, yield, tree condition, foliage, rots, lightning strikes, crown gall, and limb-breakage are also involved in the rating. Ratings are subjective but still reflect profit potential. For example, a good canopy with a good off-season yielding Stuart tree may rate a 10, whereas a poor variety like Frotscher or Moore may rate low because of low nut quality. A Stuart with no crop in an off year would still rate low even though it's a good variety. Making an orchard map will help in keeping up with what trees you remove. This will allow you to get a better idea of when you have reached the 50/50 canopy/open floor objective. When thinning an orchard, research indicates that it is best to do prior to an "on" year. Trees can also be moved with tree spades to other locations where land is available, rather than simply cutting the tree down. Overcrowded trees become stressed as their roots receive insufficient sunlight, water, and nutrients to fill the nuts and store carbohydrate reserves for the following season. A variety of options exist for opening up light to an orchard. Often the most suitable method will depend on the particular grower.

Good luck with your pecan trees!

Planting a Pecan Orchard

I was contacted by a farmer a few years ago who wanted to plant a pecan orchard on ten acres of his farm land. He wanted to know if I would be interested in supervising the complete construction of the orchard, from the tree planting to installing an irrigation system. Even though I eventually determined that I simply did not have the time necessary to assist him, I did spend a considerable amount of time thinking about the entire process. With the confession that I only almost planted a pecan orchard once upon a time, I offer my thoughts and advice on undertaking such a huge and expensive project.

If you're reading this, there's a good chance that you're still in the planning stages, or even the 'just thinking about it' stage. I would like to encourage you to consider searching out an established orchard that is for sale before you commit yourself to planting an entire orchard of pecan trees, especially if you are approaching middle age. Keep in mind that you will not see a single pecan for at least five years, and will not have a sufficient crop to even harvest for close to ten years. You will not break even on your annual expenses until years twelve to fifteen, not to mention recoup the initial expense of planting your orchard, which may come at year twenty. If I haven't talked you out of planting an orchard yet, then I remind you that you must commit yourself to caring for your young orchard diligently for the long haul. It pains me to drive throughout the countryside and see abandoned and neglected pecan orchards that somebody lost interest in years before the orchard had a chance to prove itself.

So you still want to plant a pecan orchard

Choose your location wisely. You must have access to an unlimited supply of water. Your orchard will not survive without it. Soil conditions must be considered, along with

You now have your pecan tree planted. With a water hose, soak the area around your tree. This will allow the dirt to settle around the roots and will also remove any remaining air pockets.

Your young pecan tree will probably need to be staked. Wind, pets, kids, and such can cause damage. You'll need some rope, preferably cotton or nylon, and three stakes. To prevent damage to your young tree trunk, wrap an area with plastic or rubber (a piece of bicycle innertube works great.) Then loosely tie the three pieces of rope onto the protected trunk. Drive the three stakes an equal distance apart into the ground and attach the rope.

While you sit back and patiently wait for spring to bring your newly planted tree to life, keep these important tips in mind. Water your tree frequently and thoroughly during its first few years. Keep insects off your young tree. A zinc spray is essential for optimal growth; however, nitrogen fertilizer should not be applied during the first growing season. For more in-depth information on caring for your new pecan tree, be sure to visit our other sections covering these topics.

usually just above the root system, is typically recognized as a knot or a crook in the base of your young tree. If you bury the graft, the tree will put off shoots below the graft, which will be native rather than the hybrid pecan variety. Your tree runs the risk of losing its graft. You should plant your tree with at least three inches of native trunk exposed above ground level. In other words, your graft should be about four fingers above the soil line.

While care should be taken not to plant your tree too deep, the bottom of your hole should be loosened with a shovel to make it easier for your tap root to establish itself. Dig the hole two and a half to three feet in diameter to allow young feeder roots ample room to spread. Once your hole is dug, fill it completely full of water. You can take a break as you allow the water time to soak completely into the soil. This is, I firmly believe, the single most crucial step in successful pecan tree planting.

Once the water no longer stands in your hole, if you are planting a container-grown tree, gently bump the sides of the container with the heel of your hands to loosen the dirt. Grasp the tree by its trunk and lift it from the container and gently place it in your hole. If you see that your hole is a bit too deep, scoop some loose soil into the bottom of the hole. Work soil into the hole around the dirt holding your tree in place. Tamp the soil lightly to remove any air pockets. Do not pack the soil tightly around your tree.

If you are planting a bare root pecan tree, you may need a helper, since you are basically attempting to put a one to two-inch diameter 'stick' into a three-foot hole. Have your helper position your tree in the center of the hole with the bottom of the tap root resting on the bottom of the hole. You should scoop loose dirt into the hole with your hands, taking care to position any small feeder roots in a horizontal position before covering them with soil. Once your hole is filled, gently tamp the soil to remove any air pockets.

Planting Your Pecan Tree

You've chosen your variety of pecan tree, picked a suitable location, and the time has arrived to plant your pecan tree. It's time to pick up the shovel.

Pecan trees have a central tap root whose sole purpose during its lifespan is to seek out water and nutrients in the soil, vast amounts of water and nutrients. It's important to keep this mission in mind as you plant. If you are living in an area with shallow topsoil, solid bedrock, lack of a sub-surface water table, or just a nutrient deficient soil, you might want to reconsider the idea of planting a pecan tree. Regardless how diligent you are in caring for your tree, if the right conditions don't exist, your pecan tree will struggle.

If you purchased your pecan tree locally, it probably came in a container, a 'bucket' with dirt covering the roots of the tree. If you purchased your tree from a distant nursery, it would more than likely arrive at your home 'bare root,' with no soil protecting the tree roots. While I've had success in planting bare root trees, it is important to note that the tree inevitably suffered some stress and will require additional care to pull it through.

Your first and foremost chore when your new tree arrives, whether it be bare root or in a container, is to water it thoroughly. If your tree is bare root and you cannot plant it immediately, you should dig a shallow trench and get your tree into soil as quickly as possible. Be sure all roots are covered with soil and soak the tree roots with water.

Let's plant a pecan tree

Dig a hole. While planting a tree is a simple undertaking, there are a couple of things to keep in mind. Unless you are planting a native pecan tree, your tree is a grafted hybrid variety, which means a branch from a specific variety of pecan tree has been grafted onto native rootstock. When digging your hole, be sure not to plant the tree deeper than the roots of the tree. The graft,

your yard, keep in mind that power lines that are twenty feet high will someday pose a problem if you plant a pecan tree beneath it. Your power company will be merciless in pruning your stately pecan tree into an ugly deformed mess of greenery to keep it from interfering with 'their' power line. Be wary of planting too close to your house or fence. It is hard to imagine that three-foot pecan sapling having a trunk diameter of three to five feet but someday, perhaps when you're too old to do anything about it, your pecan tree could literally invade your home. You should also be aware of sewer lines, gas lines, and water lines running beneath your topsoil. If you are looking at (c) planting an entire pecan orchard, I've included a section relating to the topic.

When to plant your pecan tree
I personally suggest you plan your planting for mid to latter February. I have read several articles suggesting a fall planting will add approximately one year's growth to your tree, but I feel this method has its flaws. First, in order for your tree to 'take root,' you will need to water it. You might not be so diligent in watering your newly planted tree when the temperature is twenty degrees outside and the outside faucet is frozen up for weeks at a time. I prefer to plant my trees at the back end of winter, giving the soil around their roots just enough time to settle before the spring sunshine and warmer temperatures bring your new tree to life. It is probably safe to plant your pecan tree until mid-April. After that, the summer heat will take its toll and your tree will struggle to survive.

With hesitation I admit that pecan trees are somewhat inferior trees when it comes to pollination. Pecan trees have dichogamous flowering since male and female flowers on a tree mature at separate times. A pecan tree will not adequately pollinate itself as a result. If you are planting only one tree, it will need a source of pollination to produce pecans. If you're lucky, your neighbor has a pecan tree that is compatible with the variety you have chosen to plant. To complicate matters, not all varieties are suitable for various geographical locations. More than five hundred hybrid varieties of pecan trees exist throughout the world. So, how do you make the right choice?

If you've decided to purchase your tree locally, it is likely that the retailer in your area will only stock varieties that are compatible for your region. Your county extension agent should be able to assist you in the varieties suitable for your location. I suggest you enquire throughout your neighborhood or if there is a pecan orchard in your area, stop by for a visit. I know for a fact that old pecan farmers enjoy talking about pecans! They would be more than happy to talk with you.

Where to plant your pecan tree
Pecan trees grow to an enormous size. While you don't have the usual problems with a wandering root system that many shade trees cause, your pecan tree will eventually reach a height of eighty to a hundred feet and spread its canopy of leaves thirty to fifty feet in all directions. If you are planting a pecan tree in

removed from its roots. Even though the supplier will probably take extreme measures to prevent damage to the tree roots, ultimately the tree will suffer some degree of stress. More than likely, a bareroot tree will take some time to overcome this stress once it's been planted. It is quite possible that the tree will lose its first year's growth because of being shipped 'bareroot.' It has been my experience with other fruit trees I have purchased online in the past that the survival rate for bareroot trees is about 50%-75%...something to keep in mind.

So, I have given you reasons NOT to buy your pecan tree from the local nursery or online from a grower located hundreds of miles away. Now, I'm going to clue you in on where you might just want to start your search for pecan trees for sale. There's a reason that national chains that include a garden center are becoming so successful...they take care of business. The very best pecan trees I have found available for sale have been at Lowe's Home Improvement Center. I have found these pecan trees to be well shaped, well cared for, fairly priced, and potted (a big plus in my book.) I usually purchase between five and ten pecan trees from my local Lowes every year and I have never lost a single tree yet. I wish I knew who Lowe's supplier is...I give them a thumbs-up for a quality product and a very fair price. You may want to check with other garden centers in your immediate area and make your own judgement call.

What Type of Tree to Purchase

for your family's use, or are you seeking to produce an income from your pecan tree?

Who has pecan trees for sale?
The most important thing to remember when you begin your search for pecan trees for sale is simply this:
(a) Purchase the right variety of pecan tree for your area.
(b) Purchase a healthy and well cared for pecan tree.
(c) Do not overpay for a pecan tree wherever you shop.

Many people turn to the most logical outlet when they want to buy a pecan tree...their local nursery. I urge you to exercise caution as you explore this source. I have found time after time that a local nursery offering pecan trees for sale generally offers inferior quality pecan trees that have been neglected. I also have found that a local tree nursery tends to overcharge for these inferior pecan trees. I recommend you shop around before purchasing your new pecan tree from the nursery down the street.

I must admit I have never purchased a pecan tree from an online supplier, but I have visited numerous online websites that offer pecan trees for sale, and have been impressed with the varieties offered, the prices they charge for their pecan trees, their guarantees and return policies, and in some cases their shipping charges are very reasonable. Keep in mind if you choose to purchase a pecan tree from a grower located far away, it will be shipped 'bareroot,' which means the tree has been dug up and all the soil

Planting Pecan Trees

If you have come to our section on planting pecan trees, I assume (a) you intend to plant a pecan tree. (b) and you haven't planted a pecan tree before or (c) you are toying with the notion of planting an entire orchard of pecan trees. If you are on this page because of (a) and (b) let me assure you that planting a tree of any kind is a simple process. If you are here because of (c) I must warn you that I've never planted an entire orchard of pecan trees, however, am willing to offer you what knowledge I have and the moral support you're going to need to undertake such an adventure. Whether you are intending to (a) and (b) or (c), we'll look at the basics of pecan tree planting.

Planning
Before you run down to your local garden center and buy a pecan tree to plant, you should be aware of what type of pecan varieties do well in your area, assuming you are counting on producing a crop of pecans. Whether you're planting one pecan tree in your backyard, or an entire orchard, the investment in your tree is itself substantial. The time, effort, and money that you will invest in making your tree grow and produce will be even more substantial. It is imperative that you plan before you just stick a tree in the ground. Not only should you consider a variety of pecan tree that thrives in your area, you should look at what you are setting out to accomplish. Do you want a shade tree that produces just enough pecans

pecan trees, harvesting pecans, shelling or selling pecans.

From tassel to table...Texas Pecan Trees has all the information you need to provide the proper care for your pecan tree.

*The author has purposely retailed this book at a price comparable to a McDonalds Big Mac Meal. We are confident you will find the information within these pages worth the price!

Introduction to Pecan Tree Care

We don't consider ourselves pecan experts, or 'nut gurus,' and we don't necessarily claim that all the pecan information on this website is 100% right, but we know it's not entirely wrong...we've been taking care of our own small pecan orchard since 1995, efficiently and profitably. Throughout our own constant search for pecan information on result, we've put our knowledge and experience on growing pecan trees together in this book. We hope you find this pecan information useful and helpful. We know you'll find it at times opinionated with a unique twist and a whole new way of raising pecan trees profitably.

Written by a pecan farmer with over twenty years of experience in growing and caring for pecan trees, the information in this book offers the home owner and small orchard operator an insight into the basics of pecan tree care. It has purposely been written in clear, concise, and easy to understand language. Within these pages you will find pecan information on all aspects of pecan tree care. From planting a pecan tree, pruning, fertilizing and watering

Table of Contents

Contents